From Loneliness to Love

Five Steps for Finding a Healthy Relationship

JoAnne Macco

From Loneliness to Love

CONTENTS

From Loneliness to Love

Introduction

I almost gave up on finding my soulmate. Broken and vulnerable after the divorce, I stumbled into a terribly unhealthy rebound relationship that left me even more damaged than the end of my marriage. The rebound from hell took me to new lows of codependency. I tolerated emotional abuse and ignored the warning signs of an unpredictable, controlling man with serious problems I could not fix. I almost lost myself in that year. My second rebound was better, but still stressful. I wondered if I'd be better off staying single. But instead of giving up, I took a break. Most likely the break was God's idea. God was working on the soulmate. I needed to work on me.

So, I spent a few years cultivating love for myself as a single woman. Eventually, hope managed to sneak into my cynicism. Hope got me to imagine what life could be like with a compatible partner, someone who would be a good fit, like when you find the right piece in a puzzle.

I had no idea my high school sweetheart would find me when the time was right. It was five years into my self-nurturing break, and 39 years after he moved away, that my soulmate returned. Now, the waiting makes perfect sense. It took all those years for us to become ready.

In the process of writing, *Trust the Timing - A Memoir of Finding Love Again,* I discovered that there were specific steps I'd taken that helped my soulmate find me. This book reveals the recipe that I didn't know ahead of time but clearly remember. I hope these steps work for you too, and that you will find that person who helps you grow in ways that feel good and right for you. You are worthy of true love, love that brings healthy passion, comfort, and joy into your life, love that comes to you when the time is perfect.

1

CLARIFY YOUR HEART'S DESIRE
(And Your Brain's Desire)

"Follow your heart but take your brain with you." __Alfred Adler

After the divorce, I let loneliness cloud my judgement. I listened only to my wounded heart. But I needed to listen to more than my heart; my brain, my gut, and my closest friends had wisdom for me, too. They tried to tell me that I wasn't making good choices about the men I was dating.

Listen to those who have your best interests in mind. Take the time to consider what you've learned, what you want, and what you need.

One way to explore what you've learned, what you want, and what you need is to write about what you're looking for in a partner.

1. Just write whatever pops into your head or leaps from your heart. Your list can take a few minutes or a few days. You can always add or edit later.

2. After you have at least ten items on your list, go back and highlight, star, or circle the most important traits. Then, rewrite your list with the non-negotiables on top.

3. Then, next to any negative statements, write the positive version. You want to be clear – not just about what you don't want, but what you do want. For example:
   - "He doesn't boss me around" becomes, "He respects my choices and asks my opinion."
   - "She's not messy," becomes "She picks up after herself and helps with household chores."
   - "He's not overly jealous," becomes "He's able to see that I'm trustworthy."
   - "Nonsmoker," becomes, "Healthy Lifestyle."

4.   Put your list somewhere prominent or special. Maybe on your refrigerator or your bedroom mirror.

Be aware that you might not get everything on your list. On the very bottom of one of my early lists, I wrote, "If he snores, it's only a little so I don't notice." My soulmate snores loud enough to wake himself - a reminder that nobody's perfect.

I did, however, get the most important things on my list, the ones on top like "Must Love Dogs." When my soulmate and I joined households, I ended up with five dogs! Be careful what you wish for.

I wish I'd made my list before the "rebound from hell" and had it posted in every room of my house. I wish I'd consulted my list before falling for/becoming addicted to someone who was very wrong for me. But now I have more compassion for people in unhealthy relationships.

I hope others can benefit from my experience. It might help to remember a few things:

- People are on their best behavior when you first meet them.

- It can take a while to know if someone really meets your wants and needs, so give it time. But don't compromise your non-negotiables. Don't settle!

- We all make mistakes. The good news is that we can learn something from every relationship. Being clear about your priorities can save you time and help you be true to yourself.

Exercises to Get You Started:

❖ Make a list of qualities you're looking for in a compatible partner.

❖ Highlight, star, or circle the non-negotiables.

2

REQUEST HELP FROM THE DIVINE

"Made a decision to turn our will and our lives over to the care of God…"

Step three of the Twelve Steps

The rebound from hell got me back into a 12-step program. Not being an addict or alcoholic, I'd come to the meetings through the side doors of programs for codependency and overeating. Step Three helped me when I felt overwhelmed by things beyond my control. It taught me that I don't have to have everything my way and in my time.

I respect that your view of the Divine might be different from mine. Your higher power might be God, Goddess, Creator, Great Spirit, The Universe, a Divine Source, or something else. The important thing is that your higher power loves you and is working for your best interests. If the idea of God or a higher power doesn't appeal to you, you can believe that I believe, and that the belief worked for me. There was a time when I wasn't so sure, but God hung in there with me anyway. It helped a lot in the loneliest years to know that God loved me deeply and would never leave me. Developing a divine relationship with one who loves us unconditionally brings peace and stability.

Turning my list over to God was easy for the first five minutes. Unfortunately, I have this habit of taking back the things I've turned over to God. I forget that my way isn't always the best way. Looking for a life partner is human, and window shopping can be fun. The problem was that left to my own devices, I can get caught up in analyzing, searching and tweaking. Was I being too picky? Spending too much time on the search made me feel a little desperate.

Have you ever noticed that feeling desperate does not feel good? It usually does not work out well. Letting go in faith reduces stress and helps us relax. When we're more relaxed, things come to us more easily, like a butterfly that lands on your finger. Knowing that God had a plan relieved some of the pressure. It also gave me more time to focus on loving myself. (See Chapter 3.)

I didn't just turn my list over to God. After a couple years of wondering what was taking so long, I turned over my desire for a romantic partner. I accepted (on my most spiritual days) that God's plan might include me staying single. I thought about all the things that single women have accomplished and the freedom of flying solo. It's not what I wanted, but I turned that over, too. I asked God to send me someone who was a good fit or take away the desire. God did not take away the desire. God was working on the plan. Your higher Power wants you to be happy and can work things out in ways you cannot yet imagine.

Exercises to Strengthen Your Divine Connection:

- ❖ Think about a time you wanted something, turned it over, and got what you wanted, needed, or something even better.

- ❖ Write a thank you letter or prayer to your higher Power for gifts of the past, present, or future. Or just say, thank you!

3

LOVE YOURSELF WELL

"The truth is, I had forgotten who I was. I had forgotten my value.… Now I had to find compassion for myself."

Trust the Timing, A Memoir of Finding Love Again

While you're waiting for your soulmate, the best thing you can do is work on YOU. Love yourself well. Nurture a healthy lifestyle. Buy yourself flowers and encouraging cards. Identify the things you love or like about yourself. What are you good at? Maybe you appreciate color, your kindness, your ability to make a great pasta salad. Maybe you're learning to laugh at yourself in a nice way. If you tend to be critical of yourself, which many of us are, this shift to the positive might be a challenge. If it's hard to identify good things about yourself, ask friends what they like about you and return the favor.

One Valentine's Day I had a party of close friends where we wrote snippets of positive feedback to each other on index cards. When I got my card back, I read some positive qualities that I took for granted and didn't even think of as strengths. I kept the card on my dresser and read it when I needed a boost. Embrace the strengths that remind you how valuable you are!

We all have things to work on. What do you want to work on to become the best person you can be for YOU? Maybe you want to be more assertive or build self-esteem. Is there a hobby you've always wanted to explore or revive? Being single gives you time to explore your likes and dislikes, to become who you've always wanted to be.

See yourself as a whole, confident individual who is fully capable of saying no to people and situations that are not good

5

for you and yes to the things that help you grow. Gently imagine your soulmate doing the same thing – preparing for a healthy relationship and becoming the best person he or she can be.

This kind of work often involves forgiving ourselves and others. Forgiveness is a process that clears away clutter. Forgiveness makes room for a healthy relationship with someone else. For the first few years after my divorce, I could only pray for the willingness to forgive. Anger had turned into a giant boulder of resentment. It blocked the path to my happiness. I chipped away at that boulder for almost ten years.

In *Trust the Timing*, I wrote about my forgiveness breakthrough: On New Year's Eve of 2010, I walked a stone labyrinth at a church. It was almost midnight when I reached the center. There in the candlelight, I whispered words of forgiveness to my ex and to myself. The boulder of resentment disintegrated into tiny pebbles that I still trip over now and then. But the path was clear enough for love to come through. My soulmate found me six months later.

Exercises to Love Yourself Well
- ❖ Invite your closest friends to share positive affirmations. You can give each person an index card with their name on top. You could also use greeting cards or make your own. Pass the cards around for each person to write something they like or appreciate about the person whose name is on the card. When the cards come back to the owner, reading them out loud gives the affirmations more power.

- ❖ Make a collage or scrapbook about your strengths, goals, and the constants in your life. I used magazine pictures, words like, "serenity," and "wellness," and photos of my children and dogs. Don't limit yourself. Use whatever inspires you.

4

FOCUS ON FRIENDSHIP

"Friends…they cherish one another's hopes.
They are kind to one another's dreams."

Henry David Thoreau

Good friends can be the best thing for loneliness. Friends and family help us learn who we are and who we want to become. We learn from each other how to work through challenges, how to communicate in healthy (or unhealthy) ways. In healthy relationships, people don't try to change each other. We can suggest or encourage. We can express our own needs. But mostly, we need to focus on self-improvement. We can get feedback from friends about this. A good friend tells you when you have spinach in your teeth, but they don't belittle you.

Who will tell you the truth you need to hear without trying to control you? Who's always been there for you? Who do you feel relaxed and comfortable with most of the time? Who helps you feel good about yourself? Who makes you laugh? These are your best supporters – the ones you need to spend time with. This can include your Higher Power and animal companions. Nurture these relationships. Reach out to them.

No relationship is perfect. But we can choose to spend more time with people who are good for us, and less time with people who feel toxic. Sometimes we have to love people from a distance.

Try to spend several months focusing on friendship. I know it's hard not to "look" for a romance. We're human. But if you date, try to keep it simple and friendly for as long as you can. I'd recommend a year. Did I do that? Not at first. I had to learn the hard way. I didn't realize how vulnerable I was after the divorce. My self-esteem had taken a big hit and I needed more time to heal than I realized.

Every relationship can teach us about setting boundaries and loving ourselves. If someone pressures you to move into a romantic or sexual relationship faster than you're comfortable with, that person is not respecting your boundaries. Keep your list from chapter 1 handy and refer to it often as a guide.

If you feel like you don't have any good friends, or people are unavailable to you for whatever reason, you can develop a support network. Observe people. Ask questions about their interests. Deciding whether someone is a good fit as a friend is relationship practice. Explore the process of making and being friends. These skills will serve you well in looking for a compatible partner.

Activities to Strengthen Your Support Network:
- ❖ Thank someone for their support and let them know you value their friendship. Call, text, or write a thank you note.

- ❖ Make a date with a friend. You could go for a walk, have lunch, or meet for coffee.

- ❖ Look into group activities based on your interests or hobbies.

- ❖ Consider a support group or volunteering in the community or at a church.

5

IMAGINE THE BEST!

"What you focus on expands."
Esther Jno-Charles

While we need to learn from our mistakes, we don't need to dwell in fear. We need to focus on what we want our future to be like. Take some time to imagine what it will feel like to be with your compatible partner. I imagined comfort and joy. I imagined the feeling of being with someone who supports me emotionally, spiritually, and maybe even financially. I imagined someone who listens to me as much as I listen to him. I imagined sweet laughter. I imagined my garage which was empty except for spiders, being filled with all kinds of guy stuff.

Imagine not in desperation, but with the lightheartedness of "maybe someday…" After years of cynicism, I finally let myself watch romantic comedies that lifted my spirits. In the movie, *Under the Tuscan Sun*, the prologue tells of a town that got ready for a train to come by building tracks long before the train was expected. I intentionally arranged two lawn chairs in my backyard and imagined sitting there chatting with my comfortable partner.

Walking on the beach alone, instead of feeling sadness when a couple walked by, I imagined my soulmate beside me, holding my hand as the waves caressed our feet. When I walked my dogs to the park, I imagined my soulmate beside me and felt grateful that he loves dogs as much as I do. I didn't talk out loud to him in public since I knew he wasn't physically with me, *yet*. But once or twice I went out into my backyard at night, gazed up at the stars, and said, "I know you're out there." A warm feeling would wash over me and make me smile.

It wasn't long after these imaginings that my soulmate found me. Or maybe time went by faster because I was happier. Anyway, the timing was perfect. Maybe somewhere deep inside, I knew I was ready. God and the universe knew we were ready, too.

We don't know when our heart's desires will come to us, but believing with a light heart brings more peace and joy to our lives. Trust the timing. Maybe life will bring you a sweet surprise. In the meantime, remember to love yourself, because you're worth it!

Ways to Imagine the Best:

- ❖ If you catch yourself thinking a lot about old hurts or imagining the worst,

  - Acknowledge the underlying feelings and focus on lessons learned.
  - Take a deep breath.
  - Give equal time to imagining the wonderful possibilities ahead.

- ❖ Look around for ways to bring symbols of love and lightheartedness into your living environment.

- ❖ Make a collage, sketch, or doodle about your hopes for the future and the love you want to attract as well as the feelings that love will bring into your life. For many years, I've made January collages about my hopes for the year ahead. It's fun to look back and see what's come true!

11

Best Wishes and Much Love!

JoAnne

ACKNOWLEDGMENTS

I would like to express gratitude to the following:

My editor: Andi Cumbo-Floyd,

Beta readers: Nicoa Dunne and Linda Warden,

Linda Warden for technical assistance with the cover photo,

My husband, David, for his love and support,

And most of all, Thank you to God
who loved me through it all.

ABOUT THE AUTHOR

JoAnne Macco worked as a mental health therapist for more than 30 years. She writes about relationships, spirituality, and hope in her first book, *Trust the Timing, A Memoir of Finding Love Again* and on her blog, "Anything is Possible," at https://joannaoftheforest.wordpress.com/.

JoAnne lives with her husband David on the Carolina Coast where she volunteers, putters in the garden, and paints angels.

16

Praise for

Trust the Timing

A Memoir of Finding Love Again:

"…an absolute treasure."

"…expect smiles, tears, and tugs at your heart."

"…a book of hope and promise."

Available at https://www.amazon.com/

www.ingramcontent.com/pod-product-compliance
Lightning Source LLC
Chambersburg PA
CBHW032136050726
47590CB00008B/3121